SCIENCE DISCOVERY

Food

Q&A

Celeste A. Peters

MEDIA ENHANCED BOOKS
AV²
BY WEIGL™
ADDED VALUE • AUDIO VISUAL

AV² provides enriched content that supplements and complements this book. Weigl's AV² books strive to create inspired learning and engage young minds in a total learning experience.

Your AV² Media Enhanced books come alive with...

Audio
Listen to sections of the book read aloud.

Key Words
Study vocabulary, and complete a matching word activity.

Video
Watch informative video clips.

Quizzes
Test your knowledge.

Embedded Weblinks
Gain additional information for research.

Slide Show
View images and captions, and prepare a presentation.

Try This!
Complete activities and hands-on experiments.

... and much, much more!

Go to **www.av2books.com**, and enter this book's unique code.

BOOK CODE

Y855712

AV² by Weigl brings you media enhanced books that support active learning.

Published by AV² by Weigl
350 5th Avenue, 59th Floor
New York, NY 10118
Websites: www.av2books.com | www.weigl.com

Library of Congress Control Number: 2013952446

ISBN 978-1-4896-0688-4 (hardcover)
ISBN 978-1-4896-0689-1 (softcover)
ISBN 978-1-4896-0690-7 (single-user eBook)
ISBN 978-1-4896-0691-4 (multi-user eBook)

Printed in the United States of America in North Mankato, Minnesota
1 2 3 4 5 6 7 8 9 0 18 17 16 15 14

052014
WEP301113

Project Coordinator: Aaron Carr
Designer: Mandy Christiansen

Every reasonable effort has been made to trace ownership and to obtain permission to reprint copyright material. The publishers would be pleased to have any errors or omissions brought to their attention so that they may be corrected in subsequent printings.

Photo Credits:
Weigl acknowledges Getty Images as its primary photo supplier for this title.

Contents

What Is Food?

Food is the source of energy that keeps people and other **organisms** alive. Every mouthful of food is like a tiny battery pack, providing power to the body. In addition to energy, food supplies the building blocks that bodies use to grow and to repair themselves. These building blocks include **proteins** and other **nutrients**.

Cooks know how to make food taste and look good. A snail may not be one person's idea of a tasty snack. However, it is a real treat for other people.

Everyone needs food to survive, no matter what form it comes in. Which foods are best for the human body? You can find out by reading about nutrition, the science of food.

How Scientists Use Inquiry to Answer Questions

When scientists try to answer a question, they follow the process of scientific inquiry. They begin by making observations and asking a question. Then, they propose an answer to their question. This is called a hypothesis. The hypothesis guides scientists as they research the issue. Research can involve performing experiments or reading books on the subject. When their research is finished, scientists examine their results and review their hypothesis. Often, they discover that their hypothesis was incorrect. If this happens, they revise their hypothesis and go through the process of scientific inquiry again.

Process of Scientific Inquiry

Observation

People around the world cook their food. There may be many reasons for this. Why do people cook meat and vegetables?

Have You Answered the Question?

The cycle of scientific inquiry never truly ends. More research and experiments may be needed to test new hypotheses. For example, does cooking certain foods destroy nutrients?

Research

Scientists study the changes that occur in food when it is cooked. They have found that people are less likely to become sick if they eat certain foods cooked, instead of raw.

Results

Scientists have found that cooking certain foods does kill bacteria in them.

Hypothesis

Scientists try to understand why cooking certain foods is beneficial. One hypothesis is that some foods have harmful **bacteria** in them that are killed by cooking.

Experiment

To test this hypothesis, scientists perform experiments. They cook different types of meat and other foods. Then, they compare the number and types of bacteria in the cooked food and raw food.

What Is the Food Chain?

All living things need food for energy. This need links them together in a series. One organism becomes food for the next in a chainlike sequence. When people eat vegetables, meat, mushrooms, or any other type of food, they are gaining energy that comes from the Sun. The energy gets into food through a series of steps called the food chain.

Plants use the energy in sunlight to make their own food, which is stored as **carbohydrates**. This process is called **photosynthesis**. With energy from the Sun and nutrients from the soil, plants also produce proteins, **fats**, and vitamins. These are stored in the plants' leaves, stems, flowers, fruits, and roots. Plants are the main producers of food on Earth.

Next, some types of animals eat the plants. Plants provide the fuel and nutrients that these animals need to grow and move. Animals that eat only plants are called herbivores or primary consumers. People get at least some of their food energy from plants.

People who dine on steaks, chicken, pork chops, or tuna belong to the next group in the food chain. This group is called secondary consumers. Secondary consumers receive some or all of their energy from eating other animals, such as cows, chickens, pigs, or fish. Secondary consumers are not at the end of the food chain. This spot is reserved for the **fungi** and tiny bacteria that feed on dead plants and animals. These organisms are called decomposers.

Flow of Energy in a Food Chain

Decomposer

Secondary Consumer

Primary Consumer

Producer

Digging Deeper

Your Challenge!

Some people think it is more healthful to eat only foods that come from plants. To dig deeper into the issue:

Using books and the Internet, research the effects that may result from eating a diet based only on plants. Make a chart listing the pros and cons of this diet.

Summary

Plants and animals in the food chain provide many different types of nutrients. Some foods have higher amounts of certain nutrients than other foods do. For any type of diet to be healthful, it must provide all of the nutrients people need.

Further Inquiry

The many kinds of nutrients in food are part of a healthful diet. Maybe we should ask:

What are vitamins and minerals?

What Are Vitamins and Minerals?

Carbohydrates, proteins, and fats are the sources of energy in food. Food also contains nutrients that do not provide energy. These nutrients are called vitamins and minerals. The human body needs several different vitamins and minerals to work properly. If people do not eat enough of any one vitamin or mineral, they can become sick.

⌄ Many fruits, such as oranges, are good sources of vitamin C. Broccoli has a great deal of potassium.

^ A healthful diet supplies most people's needs for vitamins. Some people take vitamin pills when they do not get enough vitamins from their food.

Your Challenge!

The human body gets more than vitamins and minerals from food. To dig deeper into the issue:

Research the benefits the body gets from carbohydrates, from proteins, and from fats. Make a chart of the main benefits of these nutrients. Show how they work together to help a person stay in good health.

Each vitamin has a long chemical name. To make the different vitamins easy to remember, scientists named them by letters, such as A, B, C, D, E, and K. Minerals that the human body needs include sodium, potassium, calcium, phosphorus, sulfur, and magnesium. Humans also need small amounts of the minerals iron, iodine, copper, fluorine, zinc, manganese, and cobalt.

Summary

Vitamins and minerals are part of many foods. They serve important functions in the human body. Some vitamins aid in preventing diseases. Calcium builds strong teeth.

Each of these vitamins and minerals helps with a different set of tasks inside the body. For example, vitamin A helps people's eyes work better in dim light. In combination with vitamins C and E, vitamin A may help prevent cancer. Calcium helps build strong bones.

Further Inquiry

Carbohydrates, proteins, and fats are present in different foods in various proportions. They all give people different amounts of energy in the form of calories. Maybe we should ask:

What are calories?

What Are Calories?

Calories are the units used to measure the energy in food. Energy, or calories, is locked up inside carbohydrates, proteins, and fats. A gram of fat contains nearly twice as many calories as a gram of carbohydrates or protein. Individuals must take in the right number of calories to fuel their bodies every day. If a person eats foods that have many more calories than he or she needs, that person often gains weight. If people take in too few calories, they may lose weight.

❯ People who play soccer for an hour can use up several hundred calories. They may need a healthful snack after a game.

It is especially important for infants, children, and young people who are still growing to eat enough food. If they do not, their bodies will not have enough fuel to work well. Children may not grow properly.

How many calories should people be getting in their diets? That depends on their age and how active they are. Growing teenagers and athletic adults need more calories than adults who are less active do. People's needs also depend on whether they are males or females. In general, males need more calories than females do.

Digging Deeper

Your Challenge!

Are you taking in a healthful amount of calories? To dig deeper into the issue:

For one week, keep a record of the calories in your foods and the calories you used. Research the number of calories in foods you ate. Add them up. Research how many calories your body needs when you are not active and how many calories you used in your daily activities. How does your calorie intake compare to the calories used?

Summary

The number of calories individuals take in is important to their health and weight.

Further Inquiry

Knowing what and when to eat is important. Maybe we should ask:

How do people know when to eat?

How Do People Know When to Eat?

Over the course of a day, people use up energy. Unlike machines, people cannot be plugged into a wall or have new batteries put into them to gain more energy. Instead, they eat to satisfy their hunger and need for energy.

People may feel different sensations when they are hungry or thirsty. Their stomachs grumble when they are hungry. Their mouths feel dry when they are thirsty. Some people feel weak or dizzy when they do not eat for long periods. These sensations in themselves do not make people hungry or thirsty. Their brains actually tell their bodies that they need food or water.

The hypothalamus is part of the human brain. It keeps track of nutrient levels in a person's blood. It also regulates hunger, body temperature, mood, and sleep. Although a person is unaware of it, his or her hypothalamus is doing these jobs all the time.

Hypothalamus

❮ The hypothalamus helps send energy to the body during times of stress.

Sometimes, the hypothalamus finds that there are too few nutrients in a person's blood. Then, it sends out signals to the muscles in the stomach to begin moving around, causing grumbling. The grumbling makes the person think that he or she is hungry.

The hypothalamus also checks on the balance of salt and water in the blood. People lose water when they sweat or go to the bathroom. If a person's body loses more than about 1.5 cups (350 milliliters) of water, that person's blood becomes too salty. The hypothalamus signals the mouth to dry out. This makes a person feel thirsty and take a drink of water.

⌄ Drinking water is a good way to relieve thirst without taking in the large number of calories than many sodas contain.

Digging Deeper

Your Challenge!

Sometimes, the hypothalamus is not the only trigger for eating. People may eat because they are bored, angry, or tense. To dig deeper into the issue:

Research how these emotions trigger the urge to eat. Make a chart listing other ways to control these emotions instead of eating.

Summary

A part of the brain called the hypothalamus controls people's hunger and thirst.

Further Inquiry

After the hypothalamus makes a person feel hungry, other parts of the body are involved with eating and digesting food. Maybe we should ask:

What happens in people's mouths?

What Happens in People's Mouths?

Taste is one of the five major senses. It is the way people tell which chemicals are present in food. For example, most foods that contain sugar taste sweet.

The five basic tastes are sweet, sour, salty, bitter, and umami. Umami refers to a meaty taste that foods containing a great deal of protein may have. Some people also include soapy and metallic as tastes.

Thousands of tiny taste buds on the tongue detect the flavors in food. Babies and young children have far more taste buds in their mouths than adults do. This large quantity makes their sense of taste very powerful. For this reason, most children do not like spicy foods.

⌃ Each taste bud lasts only about 10 days. It is then replaced by a new taste bud.

Chewing breaks food into small pieces. Next, saliva in the mouth dissolves small amounts of food. This allows the taste buds to detect the chemicals in the food. Different taste buds are sensitive to different flavors.

▼Taste buds at the tip of the tongue sense sweetness. Taste buds along the sides of the tongue detect sourness.

Digging Deeper

Your Challenge!

Artificial sweeteners seem to taste stronger than sugar. To dig deeper into the issue:

Put sugar, NutraSweet, and Sweet'N Low on three different sections of a plate. Dip a cotton swab in water, and place it in one substance. Put the swab on the tip of your tongue. Decide how sweet the taste is and assign it a number between 1 and 10. Rinse your mouth, and repeat the test with clean swabs and the other two substances. Create a chart showing the sweetness of each substance.

Summary

Taste buds detect the five major flavors. Taste buds for each flavor are on different parts of the tongue.

Further Inquiry

After leaving the mouth, food travels to the stomach and then to the intestines. Maybe we should ask:

What happens to food in the stomach and intestines?

What Happens to Food in the Stomach and Intestines?

Swallowing pushes food from the mouth down to the stomach. When the food arrives, it triggers the stomach muscles to begin squeezing and crushing it. At the same time, stomach acid goes to work to help dissolve the food. In all, it takes about four hours for the stomach to deal with a meal. It gradually sends the crushed and partly dissolved food to the small intestine.

The small intestine is a long, coiled, tubelike organ. It leads from the stomach to the large intestine. The inside of this tube is lined with **cells** that act like guards. These cells allow only food nutrients to pass through the wall of the small intestine. The nutrients move into the bloodstream. Then, they are carried by the blood to all parts of the body to be used as energy. Some parts of food cannot pass through the wall of the small intestine and be used in the body. They move through the large intestine and leave the body.

❮ After food is chewed, muscles in the throat help move it to the stomach.

Digging Deeper

Your Challenge!

The human digestive system includes many organs besides the mouth, stomach, and intestines. To dig deeper into the issue:

Research the parts of the digestive system. Then, draw a diagram showing all of the organs that this body system contains. Label each organ. Next to the name, list one main function that it performs.

Summary

Food travels from the mouth to the stomach to the intestines. Along the way, different muscles crush the food and chemicals dissolve it.

Further Inquiry

In the small intestine, chemical changes occur in food to separate the nutrients that will pass into the blood. How do these chemical changes occur? Maybe we should ask:

What do bacteria and enzymes do?

▲ The stomach is on top of the intestines. An adult's small intestine is 22 to 25 feet (6.7 to 7.6 meters) long. The large intestine is less than one-fourth of that length.

What Do Bacteria and Enzymes Do?

People's intestines have bacteria living inside them. Trillions of bacteria line the small intestine. They are not the types of bacteria that cause illness. Instead, these bacteria help with digesting food and have other useful functions, as well.

Infants do not have these bacteria when they are still in their mothers' bodies. Where do the bacteria come from? Infants begin taking in the bacteria with their food almost as soon as they are born. The bacteria then remain in their intestines.

Several types of bacteria live in the small intestine. One type feeds on carbohydrates. It breaks down some kinds of carbohydrates that the human body could not digest without the bacteria. Nutrients from these carbohydrates can then enter the blood and be used by the body.

❮ Enzymes in the lining of the small intestine help digest sugar.

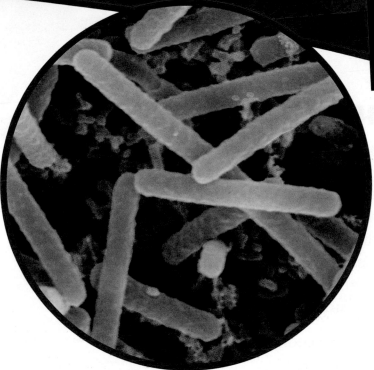

▲ The type of bacteria called *Lactobacillus acidophilus* occurs naturally in the human body. It helps prevent the growth of harmful bacteria.

Some intestinal bacteria produce important vitamins that the body needs to work properly. Intestinal bacteria also keep some harmful types of bacteria from staying in the body. They may also help reduce the possibility that a person will suffer from **asthma** and **allergies**.

Enzymes are substances that speed up chemical reactions. Some enzymes produced in an organ called the pancreas help break down fats, proteins, and carbohydrates in the small intestine. Bile, which is made in the liver, is a liquid that splits large particles of fat into much smaller ones. After the fat particles are split, they can be digested more easily.

Digging Deeper

Your Challenge!

Scientists estimate that only 1 in every 10 cells inside the body is a human cell. The rest of the cells are **microbes**, often bacteria, that are helpful, harmful, or neutral. To dig deeper into the issue:

Research microbes living in the human body. List at least three kinds of helpful bacteria, with the function that each one performs.

Summary

There are many different kinds of bacteria. Some types that live in the small intestine help the human body.

Further Inquiry

Although some bacteria are helpful, other types can be harmful. Maybe we should ask:

Why do people cook food?

Why Do People Cook Food?

Since prehistoric times, humans have discovered many different ways to prepare food. People cook it, chill it, and add spices to it. Many foods, such as sushi, carrots, and apples, are often eaten raw. Other foods, such as pork, chicken, and potatoes, cannot be eaten raw.

There are several good reasons for cooking many kinds of food. One is safety. High temperatures kill bacteria and other organisms in food that can make people sick. High temperatures also destroy some chemicals in foods that are poisonous. In addition, cooking makes tough foods softer. This means they are easier to chew and digest.

Cooking increases the flavor of some foods. It does this by heating the tiny **molecules** that are responsible for the food's flavor. With heat, molecules of separate ingredients mix together, creating more flavor. Heating also causes chemical changes that improve the smell of some foods, making them more appealing.

❮ Sushi often contains raw fish wrapped in rice.

Digging Deeper

Your Challenge!

Cooking sometimes changes the flavor of food. To dig deeper into the issue:

Try eating a piece of raw onion. Note the sharp taste. Now, eat a piece of onion that has been fried until it is brown. How does it taste? Sweet? Research what chemical changes occur in an onion when it is cooked. Compare the tastes of other vegetables eaten raw and cooked. Make a chart to show the differences.

Summary

An onion that has been cooked can become 50 to 70 times sweeter than sugar.

Further Inquiry

Cooking can be a simple activity, or a recipe can have many steps. Sometimes, people make mistakes when cooking. Maybe we should ask:

What happens if food is overcooked?

⌃ Cooking turns liquids, such as pancake batter, into solids.

What Happens If Food Is Overcooked?

Sometimes, people do other activities while they are cooking. They may not pay attention to how long their food has been on the stove or in the oven. What changes can occur in food if it is overcooked?

The heat of an oven or stove removes moisture from food. If left in the heat for too long, the food becomes dry and tough. High temperatures also destroy some of the nutrients.

Sometimes, people overcook their vegetables. These vegetables can lose both their appeal and their nutrients. If vegetables are boiled for too long, heat breaks down the molecules that create the vegetables' flavor. Many of the vitamins that were originally in the vegetables end up in the water. Overcooked vegetables are safe to eat but are not as enjoyable or healthful.

Some overcooked food should not be eaten. For example, people should throw away the black portions of burned food, especially burned meat. They contain chemicals that may cause cancer if people eat them often over a period of many years.

> Overcooked food often is more difficult to digest than properly cooked food.

Digging Deeper

Your Challenge!

Vegetables can be cooked in a number of ways, including boiling, steaming, grilling, or roasting. Which of these cooking methods best preserves their vitamin content? To dig deeper into the issue:

Choose five vegetables. Investigate which cooking method preserves the most vitamins in each of the vegetables. Make a chart showing your findings.

Summary

Overcooking vegetables puts vitamins in the cooking water rather than keeping them in the food.

Further Inquiry

Cooking on a stove or grill are only two ways to heat food. Many people also use a microwave oven. Maybe we should ask:

How do microwave ovens cook food?

How Do Microwave Ovens Cook Food?

Microwave ovens do their work by passing a special type of waves through food. Like radio waves, these microwaves are invisible. Instead of carrying sound to a radio, though, microwaves in the oven affect the molecules in food.

Microwaves quickly flip some of these molecules back and forth. The molecules that flip-flop are called "polar molecules." Like a magnet, one end of a polar molecule has a positive charge, and one end has a negative charge. Polar molecules rub against one another and create heat. The heat cooks or warms food and can kill bacteria.

Water molecules are polar. Water is an important part of many foods. This liquid helps cook these foods in microwave ovens.

Microwave ovens have certain advantages over regular ovens. The air in a microwave oven and sometimes the dishes used in the microwave do not heat up. They are made of molecules that are not polar. Microwaves do not affect these molecules. If dishes are hot, they have been heated up by the food they hold, not by the microwaves. When it comes to how quickly food cools off, however, microwave ovens lose some of their advantage.

> Food cooked in a microwave is as safe to eat as food cooked on a stove.

Digging Deeper

Your Challenge!

Microwaves and ovens cook food using different processes. To dig deeper into the issue:

Cook several foods in both a microwave and a regular oven. Bring all the foods to the same temperature, using a food thermometer to test them. Then, measure how long it takes for each food to lose 10° Fahrenheit (12° Celsius). Make a chart comparing the cooling times.

Summary

Microwave ovens heat food by rapidly flipping polar molecules.

Further Inquiry

Heating food in microwaves destroys harmful bacteria. Other substances in food may cause sickness as well. Maybe we should ask:

What causes food allergies and food poisoning?

What Causes Food Allergies and Food Poisoning?

The human body's immune system usually protects people from germs and other harmful foreign cells. The cells are called foreign because they are not naturally present in the body. Some people are allergic to certain foods. Their immune systems react to harmless substances in these foods as if they were harmful foreign cells. When a person allergic to a certain food eats that food, the immune system reaction may cause that person to break out in a rash, become sick to the stomach, or develop a stuffy nose. Some allergic reactions can be severe. Common foods that people are allergic to include eggs, peanuts, tree nuts, soy, wheat, fish, and shellfish.

Harmful bacteria and other microbes that may live on food, kitchen surfaces, utensils, and people's hands can cause illness. People who eat food containing these microbes may develop food poisoning. Every year, more than 48 million people in the United States suffer from illnesses caused by food. Up to 3,000 people die from these sicknesses.

People can take several steps to avoid food poisoning. They can keep their hands, food, and cooking area clean. They can avoid food that looks or smells as if it has spoiled. They also should not buy food in swollen cans because the food inside may have been spoiled by microbes. Foods not meant to be eaten raw, such as pork or chicken, should be cooked completely at a temperature high enough to kill harmful bacteria. Cooked food should not be left at room temperature for more than two hours. The food may spoil because microbes enter and grow in it.

> Milk and other dairy products are the most common causes of food allergies.

< Doctors put chemicals under a person's skin to find out what foods that person may be allergic to.

Q&A

What Are Some Ways to Keep Food from Spoiling?

Spoiled foods contain microbes that can make people sick. One way to avoid spoiled foods is to cook or eat food soon after it is bought. Another way is to refrigerate many foods soon after they are purchased. The cool temperature inside a refrigerator slows down the growth of microbes, such as bacteria and fungi, that spoil food and cause illness. Cold temperatures also slow down the chemical changes that cause food to go bad. A freezer is even more effective. It turns the water inside food to ice. This completely stops most spoilage.

Heat works to prevent spoilage as well. In a process called canning, food is sealed inside metal cans or glass jars. These containers are then heated until all the microbes inside are dead. This process takes place at factories that make the canned or jarred foods sold in stores. If any microbes remain alive, however, they begin to grow again once the canned food cools off. Heating the cans or jars to the correct temperature is essential.

Hot and cold temperatures are not the only weapons against the growth of harmful microbes. In pickling, vinegar is added to food. The acid in the vinegar kills microbes. Drying removes the water that microbes need to grow. Some types of meat, fish, or herbs used for seasoning are commonly dried to keep them from spoiling. Salt or sugar is also used to preserve food by killing microbes. When there is a high amount of salt or sugar on the outside of a microbe, water that is inside the microbe moves out. Without water, the microbe dies.

❯ Putting food in containers keeps it from drying out in the refrigerator.

Digging Deeper

Your Challenge!

Canning vegetables and fruits at home is a popular way to preserve them. How is canning done safely? To dig deeper into the issue:

Investigate the process of canning. Find answers to the following questions. Which fruits and vegetables can be canned? What equipment does the home cook need to can? What safety rules must be followed? What temperature is high enough to make sure that all bacteria are destroyed?

Summary

Common ways to keep food from spoiling include cooling, heating, pickling, drying, and salting.

Further Inquiry

Since it is so important to keep food from rotting, maybe we should ask:

Are there new processes to prevent spoiling?

Are There New Processes to Prevent Spoiling?

^ Irradiated foods sold in the United States must have a special symbol on them.

Irradiated food is now available. This food has been exposed to high-energy radiation for at least 20 to 30 minutes. Radiation is energy given off in the form of rays or waves. The radiation stops the growth of anything that is living in the food, such as harmful bacteria or insects. Low doses of radiation also prevent or delay ripening, sprouting, or aging of fruits and vegetables. It does not change the taste, texture, or appearance of the food. Common irradiated foods include spices, grains, cereals, fresh produce, and dried fruits and vegetables.

˅ Grocery stores can keep irradiated food on the shelves longer than food that has not been irradiated.

Is irradiated food safe to eat? Irradiated food does not become radioactive, or give off harmful rays. Many scientists believe it is safe to eat. However, some people do not want to eat food that has been near radiation. They fear that it might make them ill. Other people believe more research is needed. They are concerned about possible long-term effects of irradiated food that scientists do not know about yet. Another concern is that workers who grow, handle, and package food that will be irradiated are not careful. They might leave dirt and insects on the food, thinking that radiation will kill any germs.

Today, more than 40 countries around the world, including Canada and the United States, allow the sale of irradiated food. Not all food can be irradiated, however. Irradiation changes the taste of milk products and softens some fruits, such as peaches.

Your Challenge!

Some countries around the world do not allow the sale of irradiated foods. To dig deeper into the issue:

Find out which countries object to irradiation and why. Make a chart listing the pros and cons of irradiation. Then, write down whether you think irradiation is a good idea and what your reasons are.

Summary

Food is irradiated mainly to kill germs and insects. In many countries where irradiated foods can be sold, they must be labeled. People can then decide whether or not to buy these foods.

Further Inquiry

There are several substances that affect spoiling. Maybe we should ask:

How do enzymes and fungi affect food?

How Do Enzymes and Fungi Affect Food?

Enzymes speed up chemical reactions in some types of food. Sometimes, this is desirable, and at other times, it is not. For example, enzymes speed up the reactions that make fruit ripen and turn sweet. They help make fruit enjoyable to eat. However, the enzymes do not stop working when fruit is ripe. They keep going until the fruit turns brown and soft. Enzymes also help turn milk into cheese in a process called ripening. The cheese is refrigerated after ripening to stop the enzymes from continuing to work.

Some foods are made with tiny organisms called yeast. Yeast is a type of fungus. It produces enzymes. Yeast makes bread dough rise and is also used to create alcoholic beverages.

⌄ Different types of cheese have different kinds of bacteria and yeast in them. These organisms help to give each cheese its specific flavor.

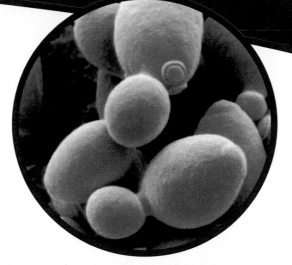

Brewer's yeast is used to make beer. It is also used to make some vitamin pills because it contains certain vitamins.

There are hundreds of different kinds of yeast. The helpful types used to make bread and wine are called sugar fungi. They feed on sugar and produce gas and alcohol. Baker's yeast creates more gas than alcohol, so it is used to make bread rise. Yeast that creates more alcohol than gas is used for making wine.

Digging Deeper

Your Challenge!

Yeast was used to make bread by ancient civilizations thousands of years ago. To dig deeper into the issue:

Research yeast. What were some of the earliest civilizations to use it? What evidence do scientists have to prove that yeast was used in ancient times?

Summary

Both yeast and enzymes are found on or in many fruits. Enzymes help make fruits ripe and tasty, but they also make fruits spoil more quickly.

Further Inquiry

Stale food does not taste good. Maybe we should ask:

How does air increase spoilage?

How Does Air Increase Spoilage?

When taking a bag lunch to work or school, most people wrap their sandwiches in plastic wrap. They may put their carrots in plastic bags or their dinner leftovers in a sealed plastic container. Wrapping or covering food reduces its contact with air.

An unwrapped sandwich is exposed to air. The air slowly causes the moisture in the sandwich to **evaporate**. The sandwich dries up and becomes hard. Few people like to eat dried-up sandwiches.

The air that passes over food also leaves behind contaminants. Contaminants are fungi and bacteria that can grow on food and cause it to spoil. Mold is a type of fungus. If mold **spores** carried by the air land on a food item, mold may begin to grow on that food.

⌄ Fruits left out of the refrigerator are exposed to mold and may spoil more quickly.

∧ Putting a sandwich in a plastic bag that zips at the top to keep out air will help prevent the bread and other ingredients from drying out.

Chemicals that cause odors also travel through the air. Uncovered food sometimes absorbs unpleasant-smelling chemicals from the air. For example, grocery stores may use bleach to clean the area near their fish cases. As a result, the fish sometimes then smells of this chemical.

Digging Deeper

Your Challenge!

Different types of mold can have positive or negative effects on foods. Some molds cause food to spoil. Others help turn milk into delicious cheeses. To dig deeper into the issue:

Research molds. Create a chart listing some helpful and harmful types and describing how each one affects foods.

Summary

Mold is just one of many substances floating in the air. Sometimes, exposure to air can harm fresh foods.

Further Inquiry

There are many reasons to keep air away from food. Maybe we should ask:

Why is food packaged?

Why Is Food Packaged?

Every home in every city throws out garbage every day. Garbage contains packaging, such as potato chip bags, ice cream containers, and used plastic wrap. Using disposable packaging may seem wasteful. In some cases, it is. In other cases, packaging is the only thing that protects food from becoming damaged or spoiled.

There are several reasons to package food items. Packaging keeps air away from food. This prevents chemicals and microbes from making it harmful or unfit to eat. In addition, some food is made up of very small pieces that need to be kept together. Imagine trying to carry rice home from the grocery store if it did not come in a bag or a box.

Some foods bruise or break easily if they are dropped or bumped. Covering such foods with protective packaging safeguards them. An egg carton is a good example of protective packaging.

❯ Many items used in food packaging, such as plastic bottles and metal cans, can be recycled.

< Some areas recycle foam packaging used to protect fruits and vegetables.

Light also has a negative effect on some food items. For example, certain vitamins in milk are destroyed when exposed to light. Milk cartons keep out light.

Although it is important to protect food with packaging, people can reduce the amount of garbage that they throw out. They can choose foods with as little packaging as possible. They can also recycle packaging materials if possible. These materials can then be used again instead of becoming trash.

Digging Deeper

Your Challenge!

Food may be packaged in plastic, glass, cardboard, or paper. To dig deeper into the issue:

Look at the types of food in your home that come in boxes, cartons, bags, and bottles. For each type of food, can you identify one or more reasons why that type of packaging is needed?

Summary

Packaging protects foods from spoiling, bruising, breaking, or being damaged by light. In some cases, however, it can be safely reduced without harming the food.

Further Inquiry

Packaging can protect food when it travels from farms to grocery stores. Maybe we should ask:

Where does food come from today?

Where Does Food Come from Today?

Today, in the United States and many other countries, most of the food people eat comes from large ranches, farms, orchards, dairies, and fishing operations. Many ranchers raise cattle on large areas of open grassland. Farmers raise pigs, chickens, turkeys, and other animals. They also grow grains, such as corn, wheat, and rice. Fishers catch fish in oceans, lakes, ponds, and rivers. Other fish are raised in **fish farms**.

World's Largest Wheat Producers, 2012–2013

LEGEND

Production in Millions of Tons (Tonnes)

- ■ 110–165 (100–150)
- ■ 55–110 (50–100)
- ■ 22–55 (20–50)
- ■ 0–22 (0–20)

ARCTIC OCEAN

U.S.

Canada

NORTH AMERICA

PACIFIC OCEAN

United States

ATLANTIC OCEAN

SOUTH AMERICA

SOUTHERN OCEAN

SCALE

0 — 1,000 miles

0 — 1,000 kilometers

N

In past centuries, people relied a great deal on foods grown or raised near where they lived. Many foods could not be kept fresh if they had to be shipped long distances. Today, large ships, planes, trucks, and trains can transport food quickly, and it can be kept refrigerated. People in the United States can buy foods that are grown or made only in distant parts of the world. Sometimes, American farmers grow more than they can sell in the United States. Then, they sell their extra crops to other countries.

ARCTIC OCEAN

European Union

Russia

ASIA

EUROPE

China

Pakistan

India

PACIFIC OCEAN

AFRICA

INDIAN OCEAN

AUSTRALIA

Digging Deeper

Your Challenge!

Are fish caught in nature better for people than farmed fish? To dig deeper into the issue:

Research "wild" and farmed fish. Does one kind have more nutrients? Is one type more likely to contain chemicals that may be harmful? Create a chart comparing the two types of fish.

Summary

Fish farming is one way to increase the supply of food. There are many others.

Further Inquiry

Since the beginning of agriculture, farmers have looked for ways to grow more food. They have bred certain plants together to yield healthier crops. As the world's population grows, more people will need food. How can enough food be produced? Maybe we should ask:

What is genetically modified food?

What Is Genetically Modified Food?

Every plant and animal has a unique code inside each of its cells. The code determines what that living thing becomes and what it can do. A gene is a tiny bit of the code. It contains the instructions needed to carry out one task in the growth process.

Scientists look for genes that instruct cells to do specific tasks. Some genes make things grow faster. Others help plants or animals resist certain diseases or insects.

⌄ In some areas, signs are used to mark fields in which genetically modified corn is being grown.

Scientists can transplant, or move, genes from the cells of one plant or animal into the cells of another one. This process creates what scientists call a genetically engineered or genetically modified organism. The added gene may make a genetically engineered farm animal grow bigger or resist infections. The new gene may protect wheat or some other important crop from being eaten by bugs. The genetically engineered plants and animals help to increase the food supply.

Genes are added to some crops that make them able to resist certain **pesticides**. These pesticides are then spread on fields. They kill weeds that reduce the growth of crops but do not harm the crops themselves. As a result, the amount of crops harvested increases.

⌃ The first genetically engineered food product was a tomato. It was sold in grocery stores in 1994.

Your Challenge!

Some people worry that genetically engineered foods may be harmful to eat. Others insist they are safe. To dig deeper into the issue:

Research the evidence and arguments for and against genetically engineering crops and farm animals. List the pros and cons. Then write your conclusion about whether foods should be genetically modified.

Summary

Genetic engineering involves putting genes from one plant or animal into another one. Scientists have created genetically engineered plants and animals that can resist diseases and pests.

Further Inquiry

Fully understanding food has involved asking many questions and researching many issues. Taking all we have learned, maybe we finally can answer:

What is food?

Putting It All Together

Food provides energy for people and other organisms. Plants can make their own food using energy from the Sun. Plants, animals, and people are linked together in a food chain. This food chain provides nutrients such as fats, proteins, carbohydrates, vitamins, and minerals. Each nutrient helps the human body to grow and stay healthy in different ways.

These nutrients also contain calories, units of energy needed to survive. People must take in enough calories to maintain a healthy weight. The hypothalamus tells people when they need to eat. If people take in more calories than their bodies need, they may become overweight.

Food travels from the mouth, where it is chewed, to the stomach. The stomach mashes up the food and adds chemicals that help dissolve it. Stomach muscles then move the food to the intestines. Bacteria and enzyme in the small intestine further break down the food. This allows the nutrients to be used by the entire body.

Avoiding Spoiling

Cooking makes many foods easier to eat and digest. It also kills harmful bacteria that cause food to spoil and can make people ill. Heating food enough to destroy harmful microbes is important. However, overcooking reduces nutrients in food. Microwave ovens cook food by rapidly moving molecules.

Refrigerating or freezing foods helps reduce the activity of bacteria in those food items. As a result, food spoils more slowly. Cooling food also stops enzymes from continuing to work. This, too, prevents spoilage. Canning, pickling, salting, and irradiating foods all lessen bacteria in them. Packaging food protects it and reduces its exposure to air and possible contaminants.

⌄ Properly canned fruits, vegetables, jams, and sauces are safe to eat for years.

Food Careers

Professional Baker

A baker is a person who works in a bakery making breads, muffins, cakes, cookies, and pies. Sometimes, a baker makes hundreds of bread loaves or thousands of cookies at a time. The baker operates special machines that process large amounts of dough quickly. A bread-making machine in a bakery can make dough that is ready for baking in only four minutes.

Professional bakers take courses at a technical school. Then, they work as apprentices in bakeries for several years to receive training from more experienced bakers. Bakers start work before dawn to have fresh-baked goods on the shelves when the bakery opens in the morning.

Nutritionist

Nutritionists study nutrition, the science of nutrients in food. They often know exactly which nutrients are in every type of food. With this knowledge, a nutritionist decides which foods people should eat to stay healthy. Nutritionists can help people who have food allergies. They can suggest healthful options to replace the food causing an allergic reaction.

Most nutritionists learn about foods and food nutrients in college. After graduation, many nutritionists work in hospitals and clinics, creating diets for patients with special nutritional needs. Nutritionists also work for food manufacturers, helping to create appealing, healthful food products.

Young Scientists at Work

Many foods spoil, or "go bad," if they are left uncovered. What is the best way to keep bread fresh?

Materials

- Slice of bread
- Knife
- Two resealable plastic bags
- Refrigerator
- Countertop

Instructions

1. With an adult's help, cut a slice of bread into four pieces.

2. Put one piece uncovered on the kitchen counter.

3. Place another piece in a sealed plastic bag and set it next to the first.

4. Put one piece of bread in a sealed plastic bag and one uncovered piece in the refrigerator.

5. Wait one week.

6. Look at each piece of bread closely.

Observations

What changes do you see in each piece of bread? How does exposure to air and to colder conditions affect each piece of bread? Make sure to throw out the bread when you are finished with the experiment.

Quiz

Today, more than 23 million children and teenagers in the United States are overweight or **obese**. Many of these young people are at risk for health problems. The Academy of Nutrition and Dietetics has conducted surveys about young people's eating habits. According to the academy, almost 40 percent of the total calories eaten by children and teenagers comes from foods with very little nutritional value. These "empty-calories" foods include soda, other sugary drinks, sweet desserts, and pizza. What are your eating habits? Are you eating the right amounts of nutritious foods every day?

The five food groups are fruit, vegetables, protein foods, dairy products, and grains. Does your daily diet include foods from all five food groups?

More than 1 out of every 10 youngsters skip breakfast. This can harm their performance at school. Do you eat breakfast? If not, how do you feel by lunchtime?

The human body uses protein to build bones, muscles, skin, and more. Do you get enough protein? Do you eat protein-rich foods such as fish, meat, nuts, beans, dairy products, and poultry?

The U.S. government suggests that half of the food on your plate at mealtimes should be fruits and vegetables. Most 10-year-old girls and boys should eat 2.5 to 3 cups (0.6 to 0.7 liters) of fruits and vegetables every day. Do you eat fruits and vegetables every day? What kinds and how many?

Key Words

allergies: physical reactions, such as sneezing or watery eyes, to substances that do not make the average individual react the same way

asthma: a lung disease that makes it hard to breathe and causes coughing

bacteria: a group of tiny, one-celled organisms

carbohydrates: substances in food that provide a great deal of energy because they are made up of sugars and starches

cells: the smallest structures that make up all living things

evaporate: to change from a liquid into a gas

fats: yellow or white oily substances found in animals and some plants that can provide or store food energy

fish farms: areas of fresh water or salt water, with barriers around them, where fish are raised for food

fungi: plantlike organisms with no roots, shoots, or leaves

microbes: extremely tiny organisms, including some germs that make people sick

molecules: the smallest particles of a substance, composed of one or more atoms

nutrients: substances, usually ingredients in foods, that the body needs to grow and remain healthy

obese: overweight by a large amount and at risk of certain illnesses as a result

organisms: individual animals, plants, or single-celled life forms

pesticides: chemicals that can kill unwanted weeds, insects, or other organisms

photosynthesis: the process by which plants make sugar from water and sunlight

proteins: nutrients found especially in meats, eggs, beans, and dairy products that are important to the growth and health of body cells

spores: inactive particles of a fungus or other living thing that can begin to grow under the right conditions

Index

Log on to www.av2books.com

AV² by Weigl brings you media enhanced books that support active learning. Go to www.av2books.com, and enter the special code found on page 2 of this book. You will gain access to enriched and enhanced content that supplements and complements this book. Content includes video, audio, weblinks, quizzes, a slide show, and activities.

AV² Online Navigation

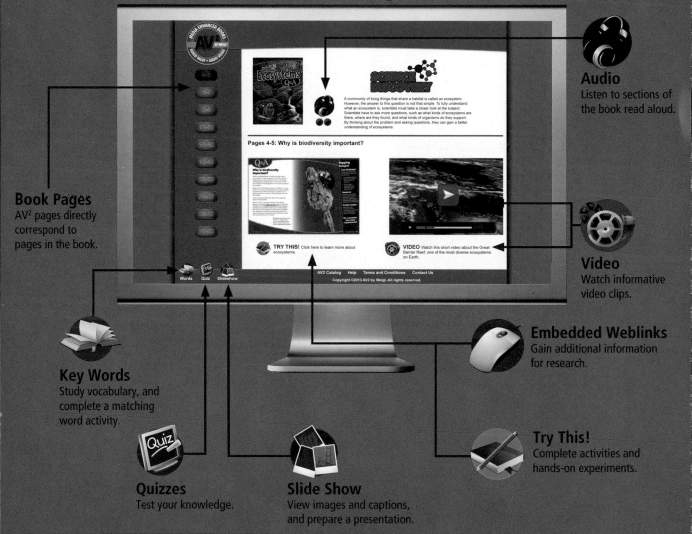

Audio
Listen to sections of the book read aloud.

Book Pages
AV² pages directly correspond to pages in the book.

Video
Watch informative video clips.

Key Words
Study vocabulary, and complete a matching word activity.

Embedded Weblinks
Gain additional information for research.

Try This!
Complete activities and hands-on experiments.

Quizzes
Test your knowledge.

Slide Show
View images and captions, and prepare a presentation.

AV² was built to bridge the gap between print and digital. We encourage you to tell us what you like and what you want to see in the future.

Sign up to be an AV² Ambassador at www.av2books.com/ambassador.